Life Up Close

Susan Brown

BookLeaf Publishing

Presentation by *BookLeaf Publishing*

Web: www.bookleafpub.com

E-mail: info@bookleafpub.com

ISBN: 9789357213462

First edition 2023

21 Days

pen to paper
stop and think
to express my thoughts
with a bit of ink.
pondering, pausing
absorbing thoughts anew
about my life and the things i do.
to pause and give a bit of time
to speak the things shuffling about in my mind.
twenty one days of thoughts that spin
join me on this journey as it begins.

This is the Day!

Hooves move through leaves so crisp
heart full; so much was missed-

Surgery recovery was way too slow
finally better, so ready to go-

Set the alarm for a sunrise ride
excitement feels like Christmas inside!

Then- wide awake and feeling delighted
no alarm needed- I'm just too excited!

Pull on those old familiar riding jeans,
scuffed up boots- bundle up by all means!

Slip on the quilted coat that's red
then grab the lead rope- just a slip over his head.

Walk through the pasture wet with dew-
you know...I think my horse has been ready to
go too!

Dusty brushing- his coat's getting long!

Then saddle up....

Step up....

back
where
I
belong.

Then a sigh of relief
with a feeling of joy
I'm finally back to riding on my favorite boy!

Hey Alexa Play~

Rock~ I'm feeling like a rebel while I smirk-
Beatles~ gotta have a song while I work.

Vocal Choral Songs~ sit in my feelings while they beseech-
Earth, Wind & Fire~ Road trip! We're going to the beach!

Lo-Fi~ the day's going well but I need some sound-
Best of the 80's~ takes me to high school and memories come round.

Marching Band Music~ it's football season-
Ray Conniff Singers~ when traditional Christmas is the reason.

Van Halen~ for the summertime-
Best of Chicago~ remembering first dating that man of mine.

Disney Music~ got my kids in the car-
Broadway Musicals~ when I want to belt like a star!

E.L.O.~ for the perfect morning drive-
Worship Music~ to praise God for this life!

Classic Sousa Marches~ it's the 4th of July-
Patsy Cline Songs~ breakup songs for a good cry.

Brandenburg Concertos~ for Sunday morning relaxing-
Big Band Jazz~ just perfect for dancing!

Music~ that companion of mine and great friend-
available for all moods of life with comfort to lend.

that dog

that dog- she annoys me so
dragging my chair to and fro
chewing cushions
gnawing legs of my table
do i give her away as soon as i'm able?

drags out the garbage
chews the faucet cover
I really need to trade this dog for another.

eating the water hose
digging in the flowerbed
"Stop!" i exclaim, but she doesn't heed what i said.

I get so darn mad- i sure can't deny
but then she looks at me with those soft loving eyes......
oh well

i guess

I'll let

sleeping dogs lie.

real talk

She opens her mouth to speak
sharing thoughts of a life of past mistakes
to impart lessons of pain and heartache
to give warning to the one she loves.

She closes her mouth
wanting to show respect
but not really caring...
pretend to listen.

She bares her soul, her problems
her failures
with the desire to not
have history repeated.

She sighs as it is over
the lecture- the endless talking
time to live her life
who else could know her better than herself?

She exits the room
feeling squeezed, bruised, worn
did she speak enough...
too much?

She briskly huffs away but then pauses when she sees her weeping~
goes back to the room where the words spilled out
and stops to stroke her soft grey hair

And maybe........

the feelings of feeling i

blessings in my hands~

pages of a new book
a smooth stone worn by the river
a dusty marshmallow dropped into hot chocolate
torn wrapping paper from the gift.

the handle of my coffee pot
fuzzy warm mittens
dirty hands on a wet bar of soap
the hammer in my hands as the project begins.

the rough coat of my dog
cool metal of my French horn
the doorknob to my classroom as a new day
begins
a smooth handrail that guides me upstairs.

the button of the camera as it clicks the memory
soft dough between my fingers
a thin hook on the fragile ornament
the soft purr vibrations from my cat as I stroke
her fur.

piano keys obeying my finger's commands

fingers brushing stubble on my husband's face
the steering wheel as a road trip begins
a pencil as I begin to write.

hands touch; heart soars.

the feeling of feelings ii

blessings under my feet~

the grit of the sand

thick plushy socks

walking barefoot through grass

the foot massage during my pedicure

the firm flat stone giving footing up the
mountain trail.

feet feel; heart full.

the feeling of feelings iii

blessings on my face~

a horse's velvety muzzle

the breeze on a hot summer day

the skin of a baby

creamy makeup that hides the flaws

warm sunshine

soft cat cuddles

slick wet sunscreen for my pale skin

cheek to cheek nuzzles with my kid

let's face it, these are good feelings.

the feeling of feelings iv

tasting blessings~

a fork carrying a savory bite

minty toothpaste erasing morning breath

steamy hot tea swirling

creamy chocolate pudding

gum to arrest garlic breath

cold ice cream melting on my tongue

biting into the perfect firm apple

~a mouthful of grateful

the feeling of feelings v

blessings on my skin~

fresh clean crispy sheets

a steaming hot bath

the dress that makes me look thinner

the warmth of a campfire when i can see my
breath

a masseuse's hands commanding the pain to
leave

summer ocean water caressing my body

being as one loping with my horse

snow angel dust from the rare southern snow

the tight embrace from a loved one

~these things bring joy within my skin

a daily gift

your presence in the present
is the best present.

aroma vacation

No touch or taste it tells
I go on a journey with these things that I smell~

Sunscreen takes me to the beach
Smoky campfires to Thanksgiving in Tennessee
Fresh cut pine trees- to family Christmas
traditions
A new box of crayons~ the big 64 sharpener
box- every kid's wishin.

Machine oil puts me in the summer rollercoaster
line
Green apple Jolly Ranchers given by the church
bus driver so kind
A new can of Playdoh- making roly poly snakes
on a platter
Rain on hot pavement~ getting stuck outside and
it doesn't matter.

Summer weeds~ staying out past dark to play
Diesel exhaust~ takes me on the band bus to
games far away.
Face buried in a horse's coat~ returns me to
riding for the first time

Fresh cut grass~ running barefoot through the
yard feeling sublime.

These take me to a place I don't ever have to
touch or see
~a great scent can sure bring lots of joy to me!

cheers

hear the jerking sound
it's still dark around
snooze button goes back down

eyes close- seven minutes
alarm blares-it's day- begin it
no- one more snooze- but that's the limit

one more time it sounds; get up
make some coffee, fill my cup
way too early
but bottoms up.

breathe it in

air crisp
leaves crunch
love this season a whole bunch

falling leaves
pure blue sky
take a walk, heart magnified

wish I could save in a bottle
this awesome day
and open it up in winter
some way.

sound bite i

fires that pop

fireworks that go boom
the sound of my cat sneaking into my room

the splash of a dive

the jingle of a holiday bell
the orchestra tuning a piece I know well

hooves that gallop

phone ringing for a call long-awaited
laughter of a child is always appreciated

sails unfurling

the timer announcing dinner is done
the treadmill timer saying I can stop my run

the click click of sexy new shoes

Popcorn popping in the microwave
the buzz of my husband's razor while he shaves

a shout of "touchdown" for my favorite team

my engine revving on the interstate
forks scraping the last of the dinner plate

the Dolby stereo demo before the blockbuster
begins

the waves of the sea as they lap at the shore
or the scritch scratch in the sand where walking's
never a chore

the comfort to hear "it was only a dream"

the click of a pen when the contract gets signed
crickets and frogs~ summer concert sublime

the roaring of a mighty waterfall

grandad saying grace at the holiday table
winds rustling leaves of the red fall maples

~sweet sublime savory symphonies of delight

Content with our Content

too many things in this room
collecting dust; memories fading too soon
the trinket once so treasured
has no worth now to be measured.

just because grandma loved it so~
does that mean it can't go?
why do we hold on to all these things
the ceramic bird with faded wings.
the cupboard holds the chipped plate in back
the china cabinet with the "good dishes" stacked.
the tatted lace, the knitted clothes
did we even notice any of those?
costume jewelry seldom worn
a card for mom from the day I was born.
and books...oh the books...dusty covers all faded
we think "ll re-read them," but those thoughts
are jaded.
the closets overstuffed and full of clothes
and the shoes- can we fit into all of those?

why do we save then buy and buy
we should give
self-control
a try.

sound bite ii

a baby's cry as she enters the world
a Veteran's Day flag in the wind unfurled

ice clinking in a glass on a hot summer's day
the sound of the boat speeding across the cool
blue bay

a heartfelt sigh during a needed embrace
the pop of a cork as we celebrate

a big breath that puffs while he makes a birthday
wish
lines that zing from the reel when you land the
big fish

bacon sizzling hot in the pan
keys in the lock coming home to my man

scromp scromp through the fresh fallen snow
taking off in a plane and leaving the town below

gathering sounds such as these
sure puts a tired heart at great ease.

church day rescue

late as always
slip in invisible while everyone's prayin
sit on the plushy pew cushion
and let out of subdued sigh of exasperation.

the prayer ends
the music begins- a beckoning to my tired heart
to pump on-
to recalibrate.

the roughness is soon coated with songs that
remind me
of who HE is and who i'm not
of what He did,
can do,
will do,
does do.

and the roughness melts and slips into the floor
as the
sweetness and goodness and love
from the One who comforts
floods my soul.

Eyes closed, I sing to my best love
to the one who has never left
and who's never meant anything but good for
me-
to the One who always listens
and gives peace during chaos.

and once again, tears fall-
slipping-
though eyes tightly closed.

an ever-so-slight flow
of gratitude offered to the One
who always rescues.
at just the right time.

I believe in you.

If only you would let me in.

Not My Turn

as my daily routine begins,
I turn on the news and see the devastation from
the storm
in that town not too far from me.
Today, it wasn't my turn.

I eat my breakfast that I can taste
I drink my coffee that I didn't spill
I get a shower with warm water and use
electricity to run my hairdryer.
Today, it wasn't my turn.

I get in the car to go to work.
The car runs.
The tires are good, the motor chugs along.
No one pulls out in front of me.
Today, it wasn't my turn.

I walk into work with legs that both move
I open the door with arms that both work
I see the time clock with eyes that can observe
and I hear a friend say hello.
Today, it wasn't my turn.

I return to a home that is heated and lit
I enjoy dinner with my family,
purchased with money that I had enough of
I stroke the silky hair of my daughter as she sits
in my lap.
Today, it wasn't my turn.

But tomorrow, it will be.

The accident occurs, and in one second, life is
never the same.
The unthinkable moment of choosing a coffin to
hold your child,
The searing pain of a parent's loss as there is an
empty chair at the table.
Today, it was my turn.

It's a long turn,
so Today, we get through it.
and the fuel
that sustains
is the memory of the days that we had grace.

When the blows of life come, why are we
shaken and surprised?
If it's not our turn today, shouldn't we celebrate?
Why do we not ponder the odds of the everyday
lottery life of blessing?

As the sun goes down on our "not today" did we realize the gift that we had?

I know tomorrow I will probably awaken.

I don't know if it will be my day.

So until then, I choose to strive to live with no regrets.

To say "I love you," and" I'm sorry."
To stop the busyness and see the people right in front of me.
To figure out what's important and what is simply not.
To make every "not my day" the "best day"

And to be glad that on this day, it's not my turn.

www.ingramcontent.com/pod-product-compliance
Lightning Source LLC
Chambersburg PA
CBHW051752130826
49812CB00033B/1113
* 9 7 8 9 3 5 7 2 1 3 4 6 2 *